I0473230

ISBN:9780692740415
ISBN-0692740414

DEDICATION

This book is dedicated to my dear husband, Roy Yarbrough. You have made our life's adventure amazing and fun. Thank you for "getting" me.

And to my kids, Mellon, Molly, Tranifer and Cari: thank you for listening to my "songs", all these years, even though you had little say in the matter.

I love you all.

My Dear Fiber Friends,

This coloring book came about as a response to the question: "Where are all the fiber animal coloring books?" This was asked on several of the social media "fiber" groups I attend. In response, I looked and found none. That started me thinking and brewing and stewing and inevitably, drawing.

Now, this book is by no means an exhaustive showing of our fiber animal friends, but is more of a respectable representation. Some are included just because I WANT to spin or felt their fiber, not because I have or even believe that it is a real possibility.

I am an artist. I love many different media and the fiber arts ensnared me instantly. I was taught to knit and crochet as a child. Later in life, I took up spinning, then traditional felting, followed by needle felting...holy cow, I admit it, my name is Julie, I am a fiber addict.

Natural fibers make my heart sing. The sight, the touch, the smell... before, during and after washing and processing, are ambrosia. I love the feel of the fibers as they slip through my fingers when I spin, when I lay them out for felting and when I knit or crochet with the handspun I have made.

While immersing myself in the fiber arts, I have never abandoned my early love of drawing and painting. A serious desire to combine the media that I love resulted in this coloring book.

The verse, herein, I must say, is mostly nonsense, mostly, but not all, my own original nonsense and something I adore and perpetuate.

I hope you enjoy these drawings, dear friends, as much as I enjoyed creating them.

Blessing and peace,

Julie Yarbrough
Kick the Moon Studio
West Baldwin, Maine

ACKNOWLEDGMENTS

I would like to acknowledge my dear friend, Janet Conner, for many years of encouragement and dedication as a friend, mentor, incredibly talented artist and successful businesswoman. Your love, help, friendship, wisdom and willingness to share your talent have meant the world to me.

And to my loving, supportive, creative sister, Amy Bryant Kelly, an artist in her own right, and my first art teacher and critic. Thank you for always lending me your ear, your eye, your heart, your mind and your hands. May we continue to create beauty for many, many more years.

ALPACA AND LLAMA ALWAYS LOVE THEIR MOMMA!

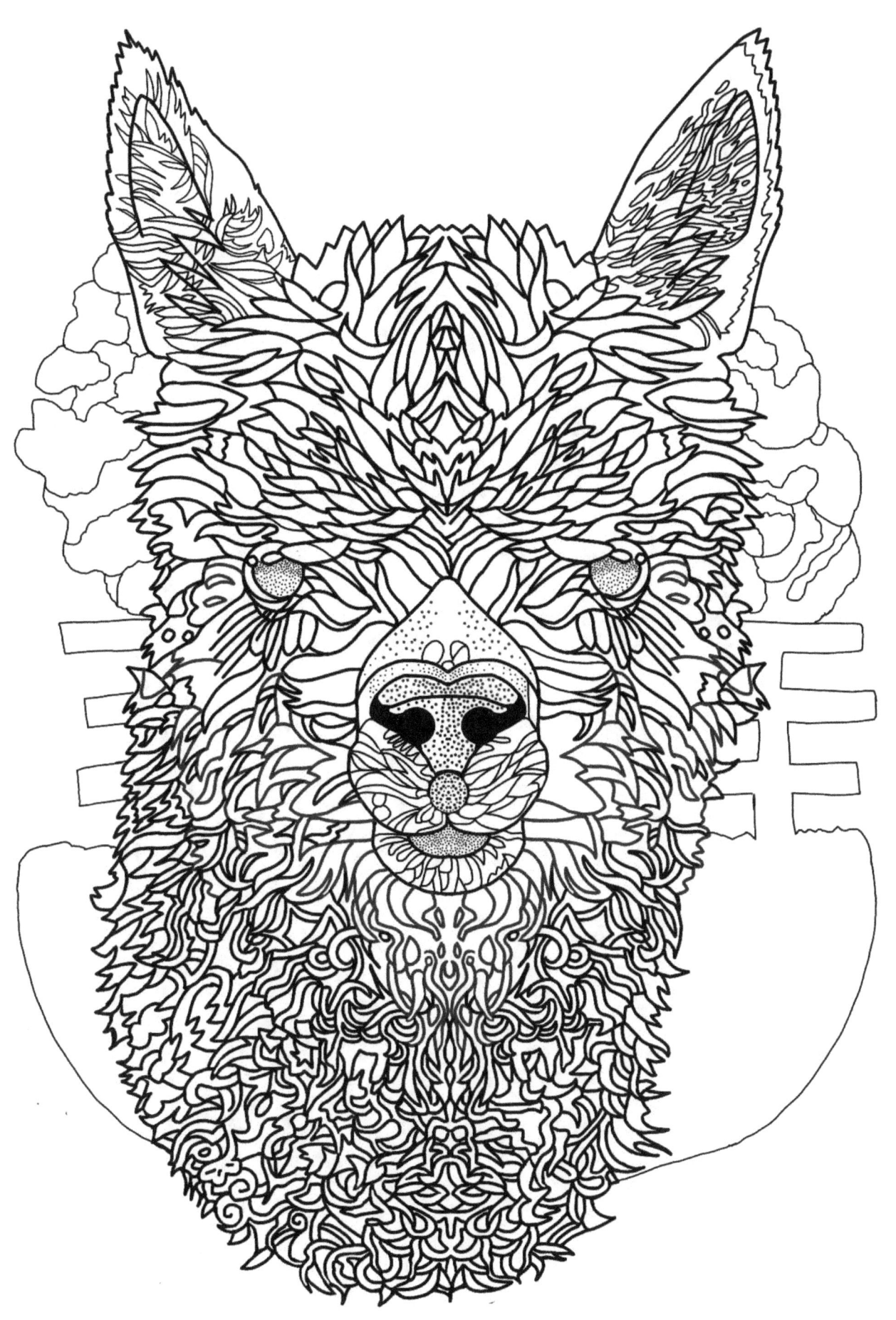

CAN YOU MAKE A SWEATER FROM A BEAR? YES, IF YOU'RE CAREFUL AND ONLY USE HIS HAIR.

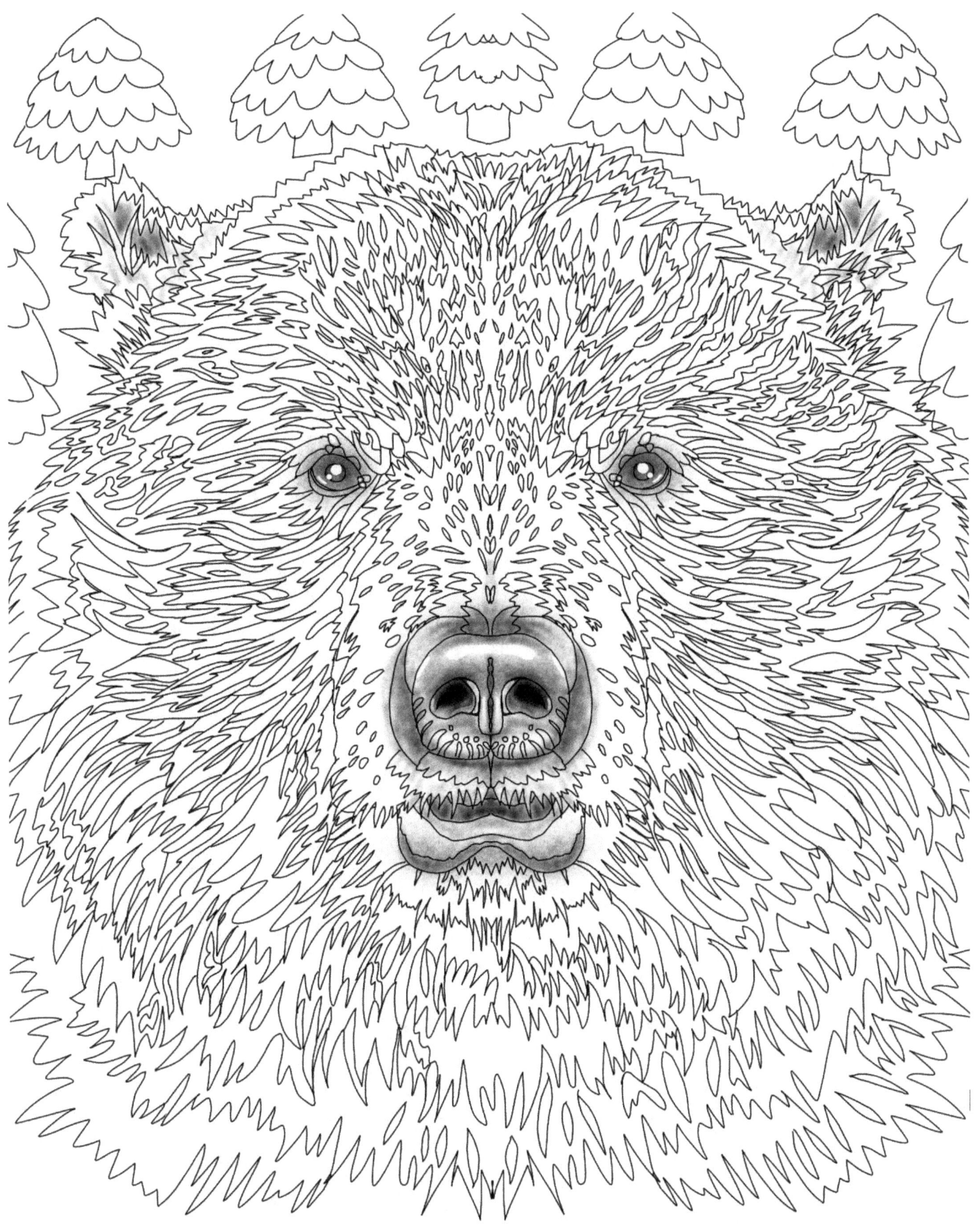

OH, THE BUFFALO ROAM
'CROSS THEIR WILD
PRAIRIE HOME, THEY
EACH EAT THEIR OWN
WEIGHT IN A DAY!
AND SELDOM IS HEARD,
"HEY YOU! PICK UP
THAT TURD!" CUZ IT
AIN'T SUCH A NICE
THING TO SAY.

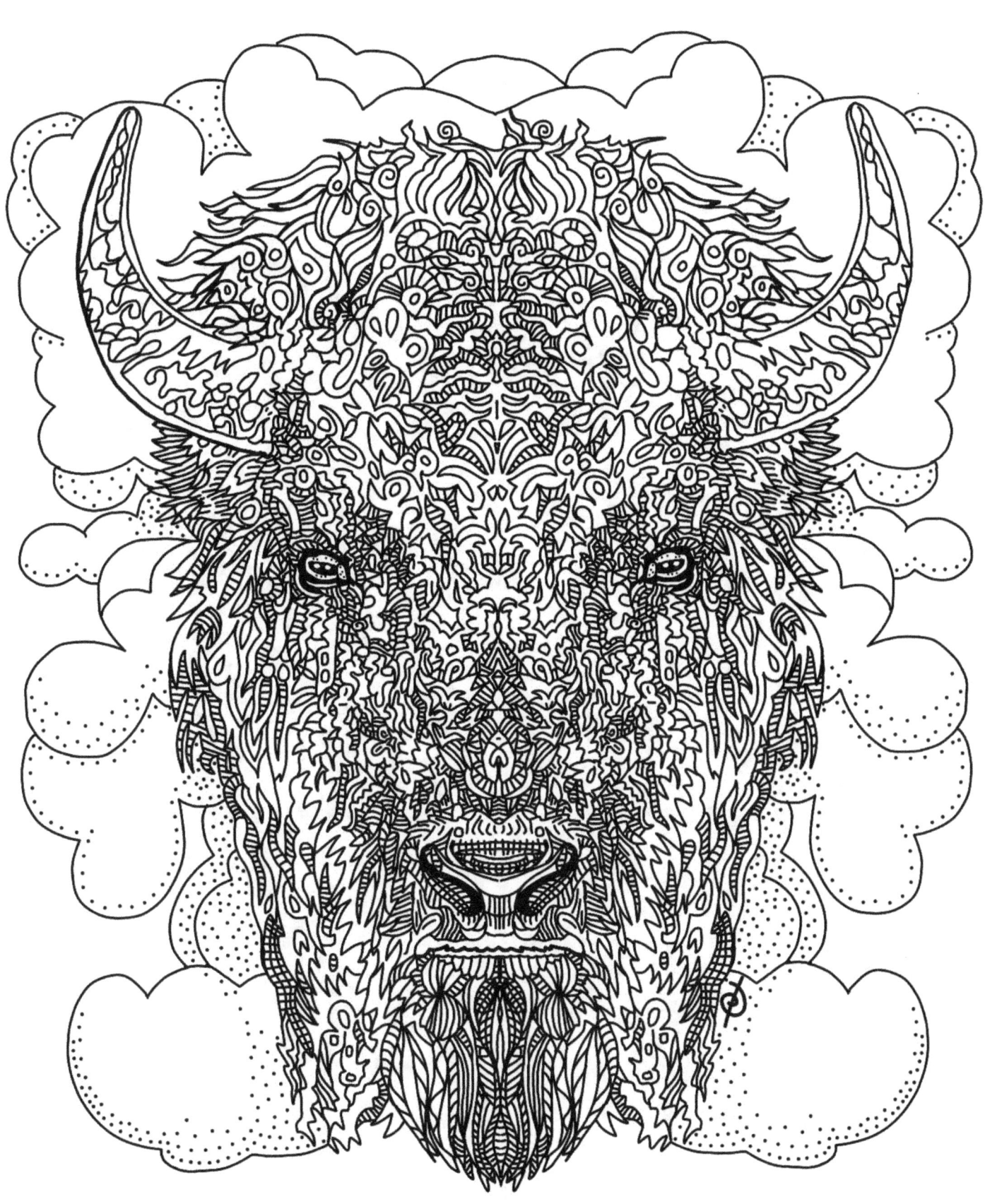

LITTLE, FLUFFY BUNNIES,
SITTING IN A ROW.
SHH, THEY ARE SLEEPING,
PLAY CATCH·A·TOE.
ONE, FOR THE MARKET,
TWO, FOR THE PEN,
THREE, FOR THE SPINNER,
FOUR, SHE WILL SPIN
ALL OF THE FUZZES
IN·TO SOFT YARN,
FIVE, WE WILL KNIT THEM,
ALL WILL BE WARM.

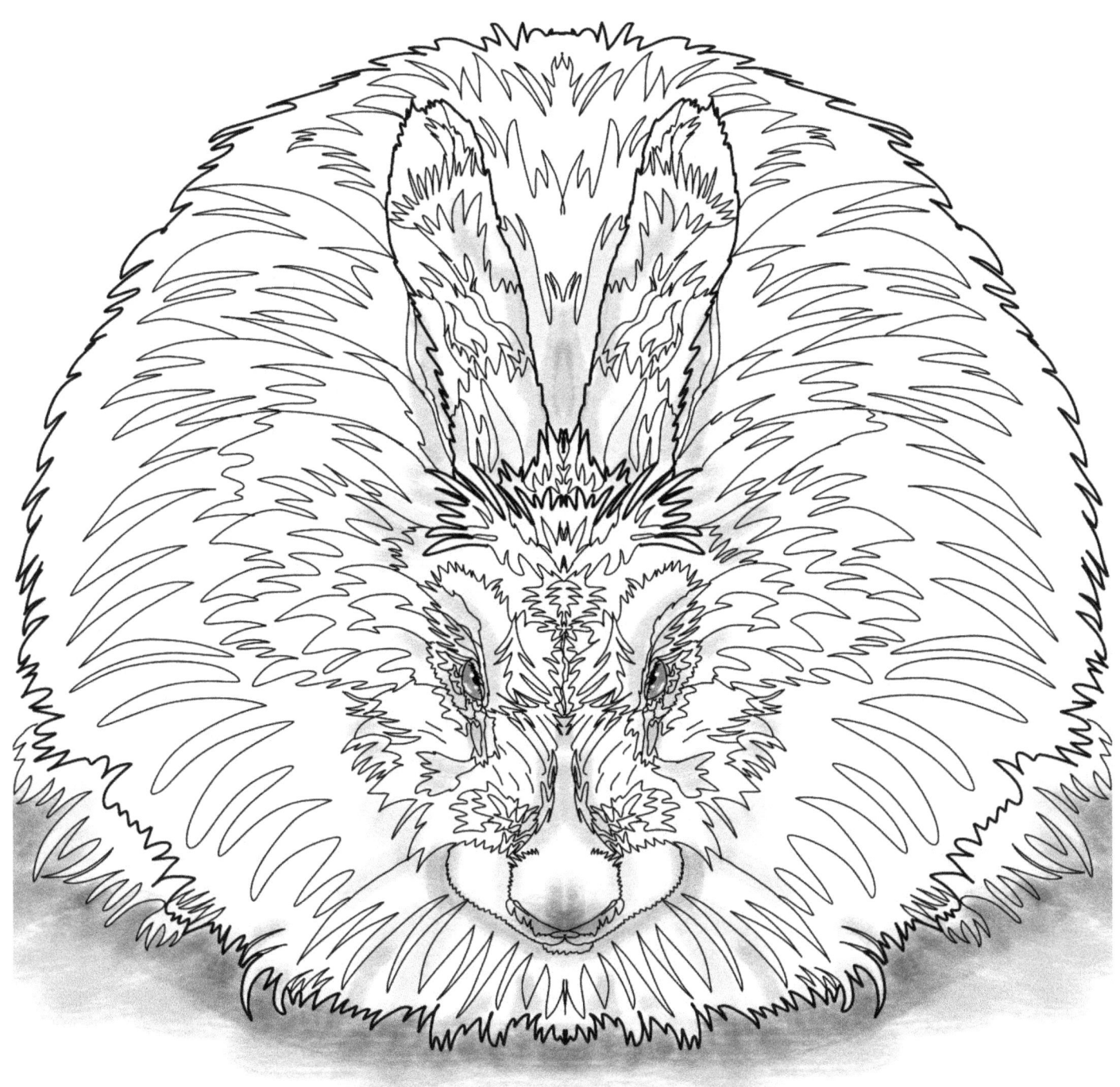

"WHY DOES THE CAMEL SMILE? BECAUSE SHE KNOWS THE HUNDREDTH NAME OF GOD."

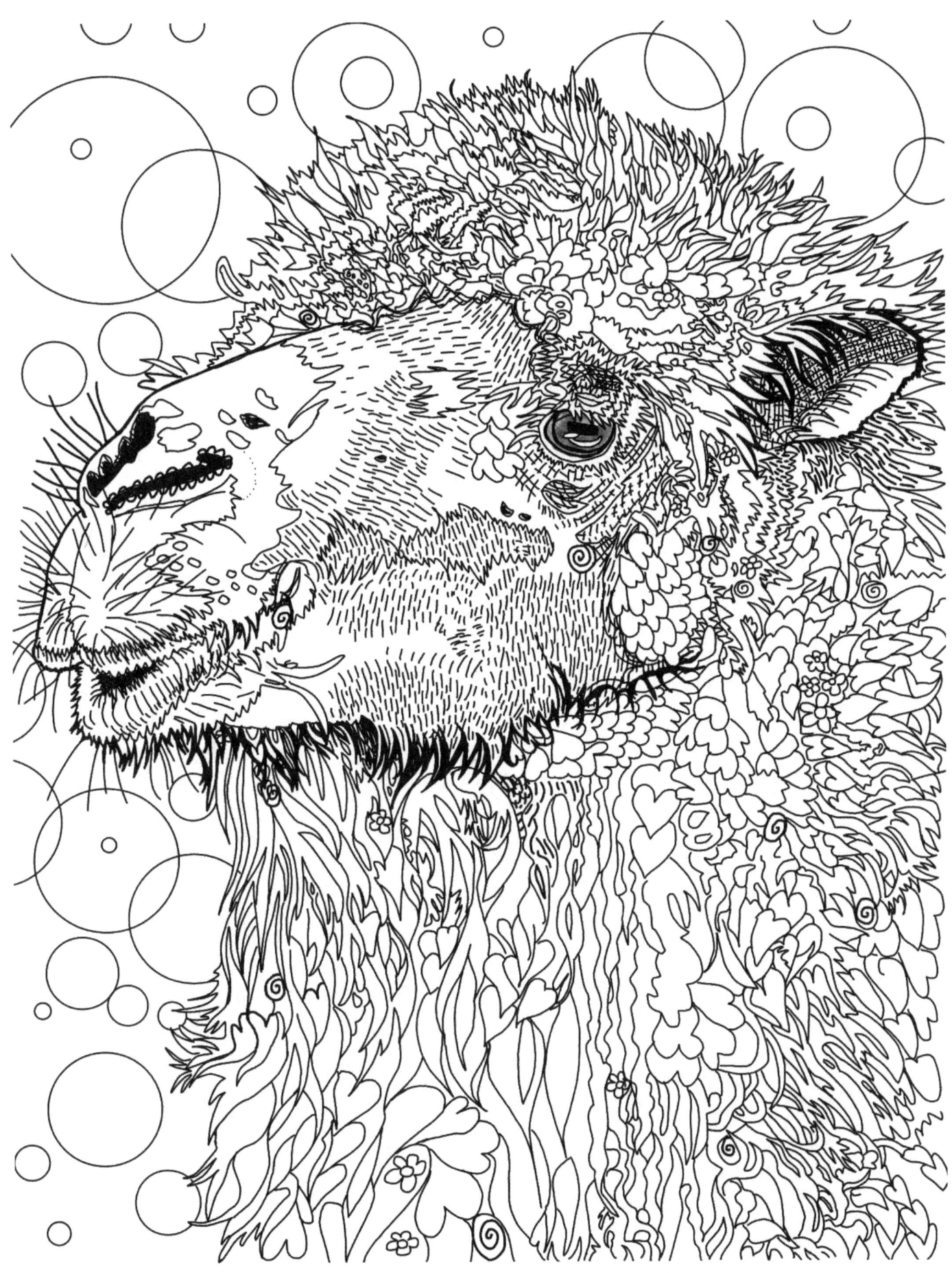

QUIETLY, THE CAT CREPT IN, CRAPPED, CREPT OUT.

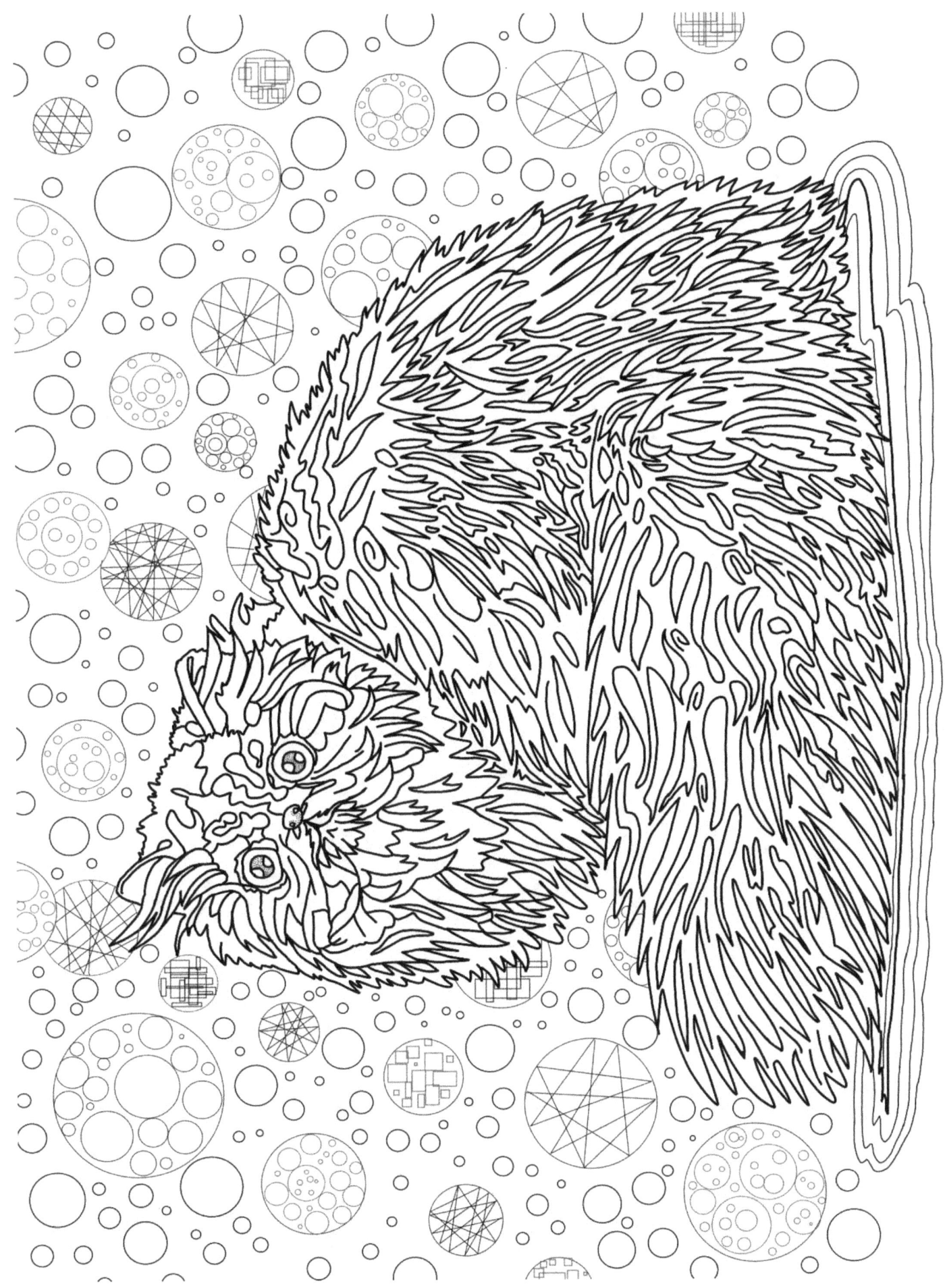

WHEN A DOG LOVES YOU, HE IS JUST BEING A DOG. WHEN A CAT LOVES YOU, IT IS BECAUSE SHE KNOWS YOUR SECRETS.

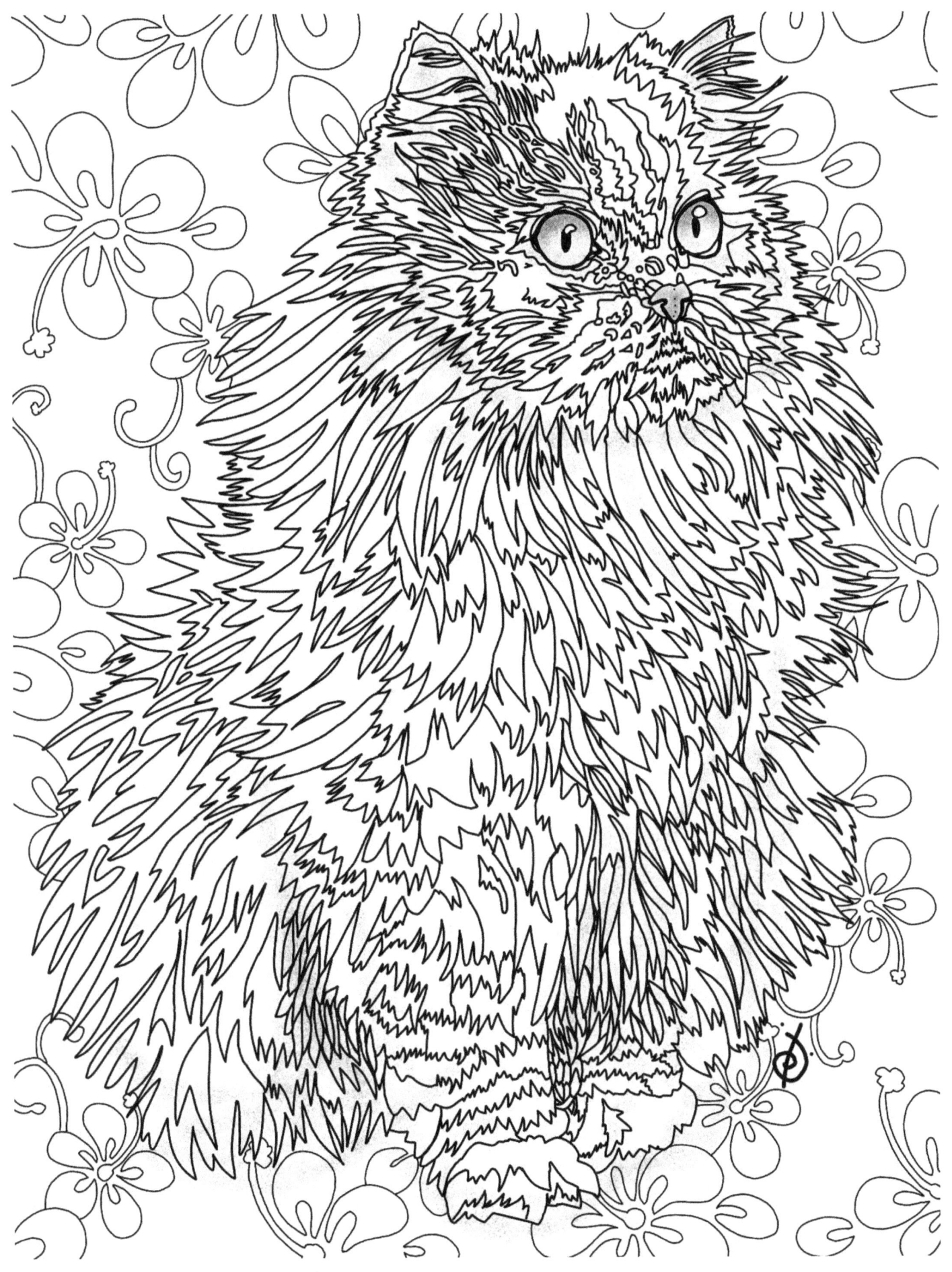

HAVE YOU ENCOUNTERED THE LITTLE DOG'S BARK? IT IS BOLD AND COURAGEOUS BY DAY OR BY DARK.

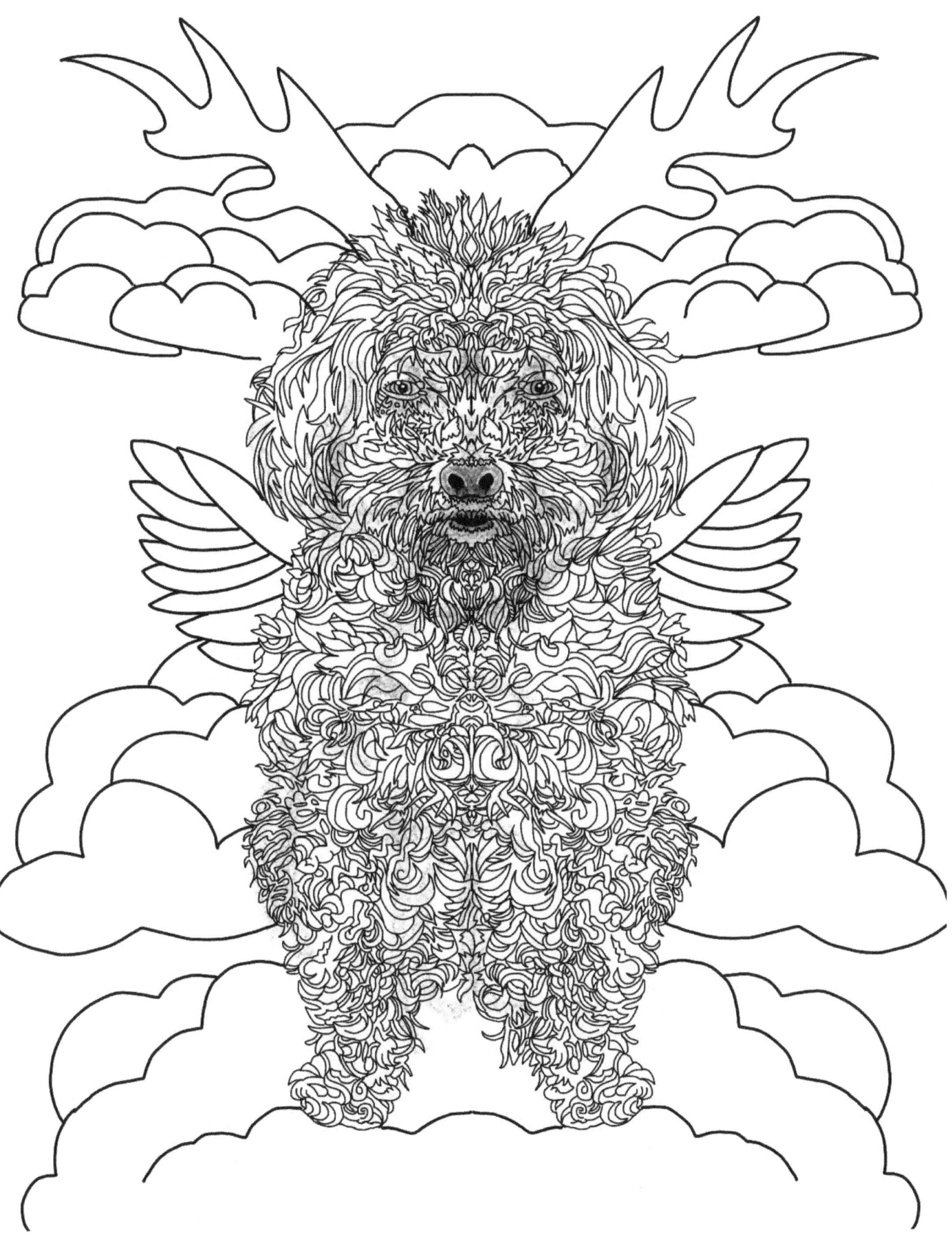

WHAT DID THE FOX SAY!?

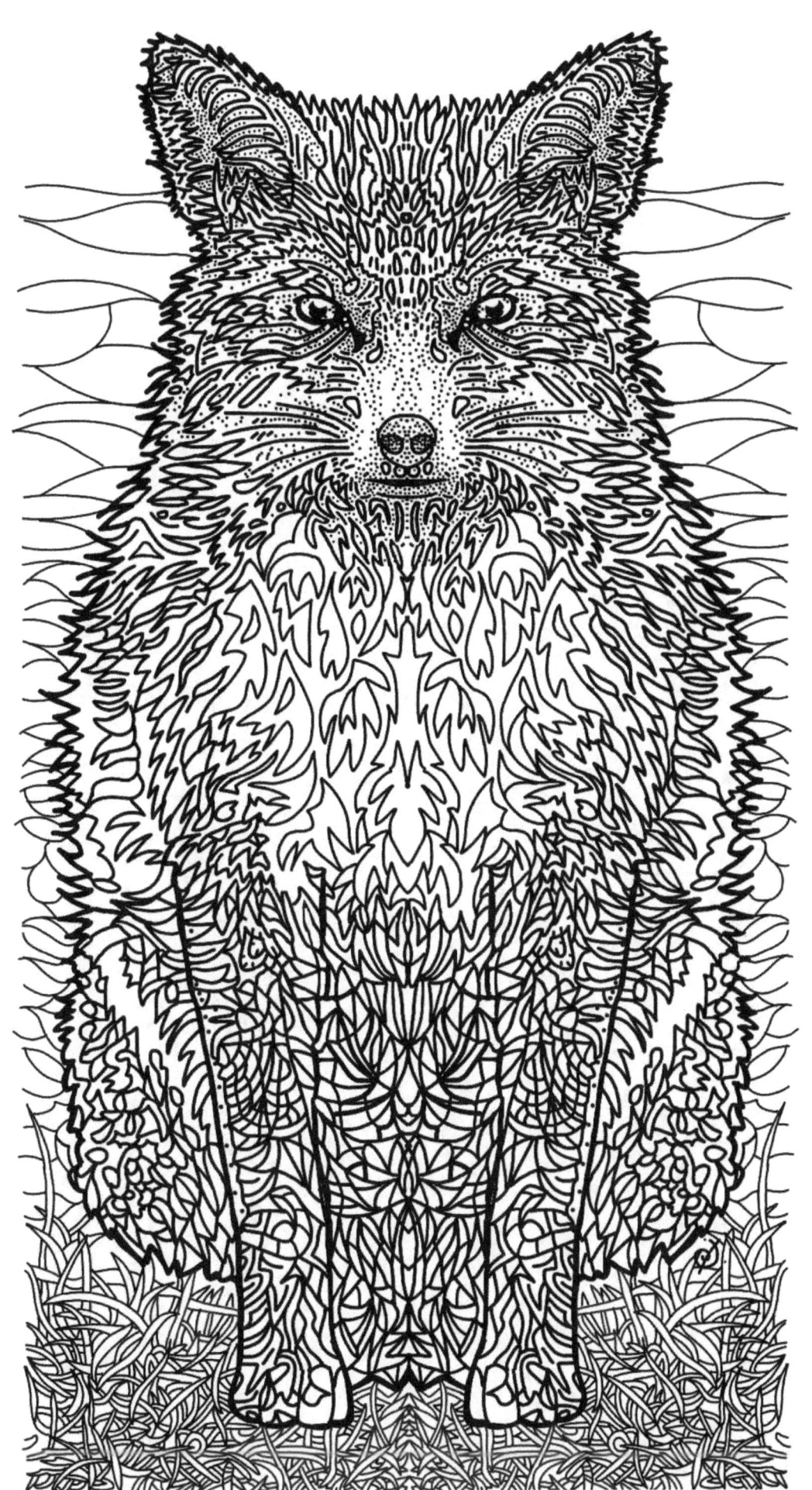

GOATS ARE LOVELY CREATURES. GIVEN HALF A CHANCE, THEY WILL TAKE OVER THE WORLD.

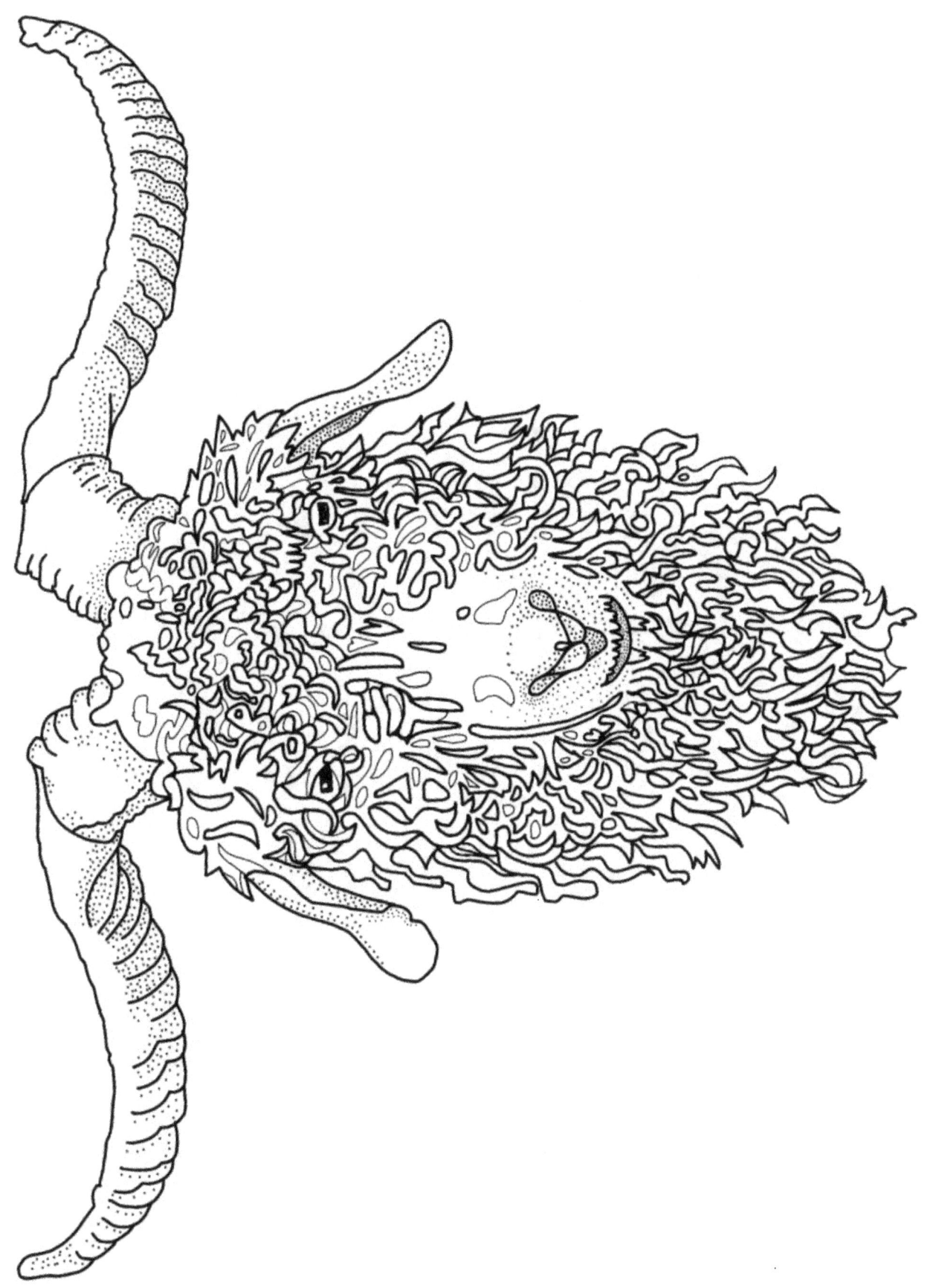

THE GUINEA PIG IS FULL OF GLEE, FIRST, HE'LL SQUEAL, THEN, HE'LL PEE.

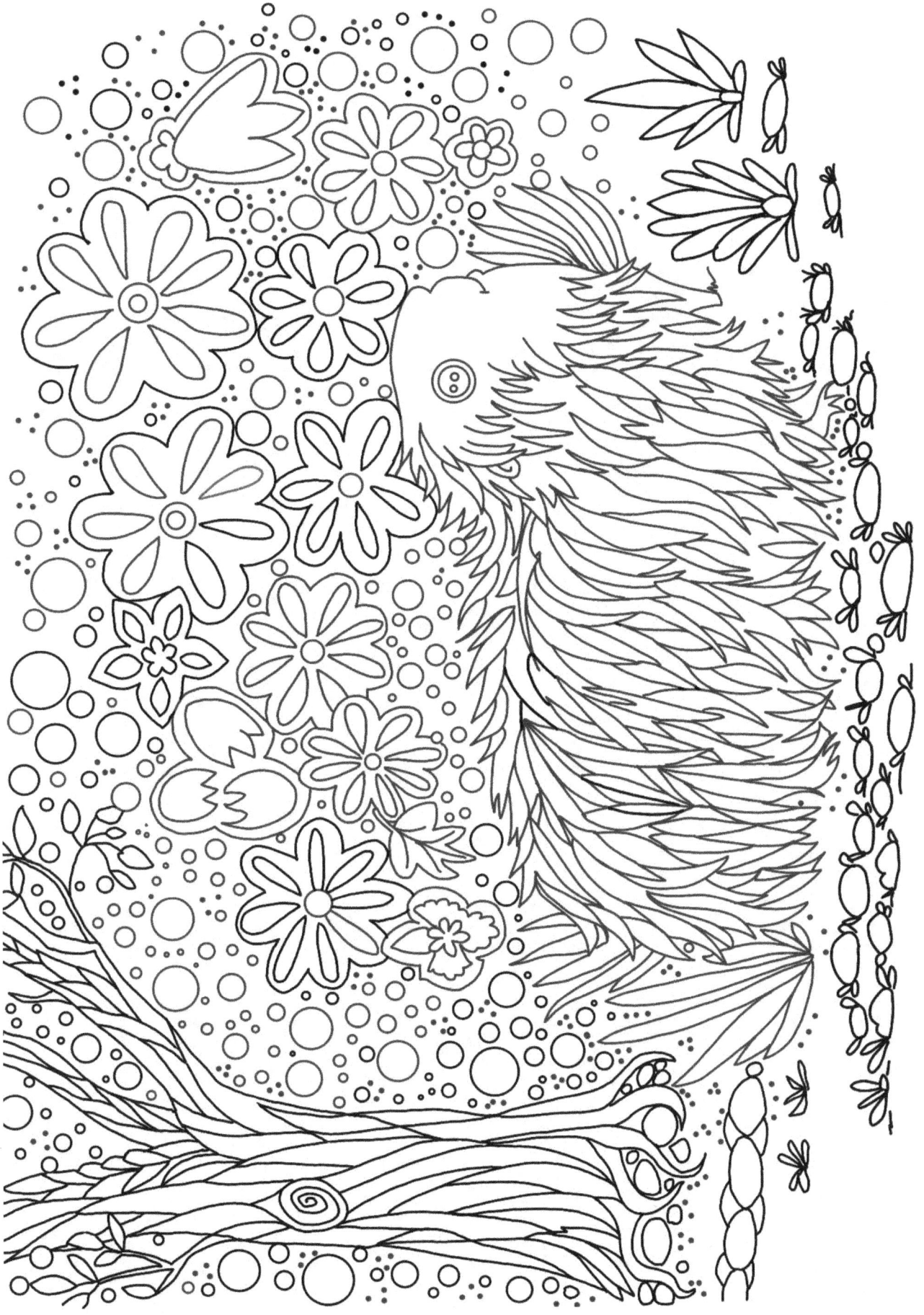

HAVE YOU MET
THE GUANACO?
I HEAR THEY'RE
NICE, AS
CAMELIDS GO.

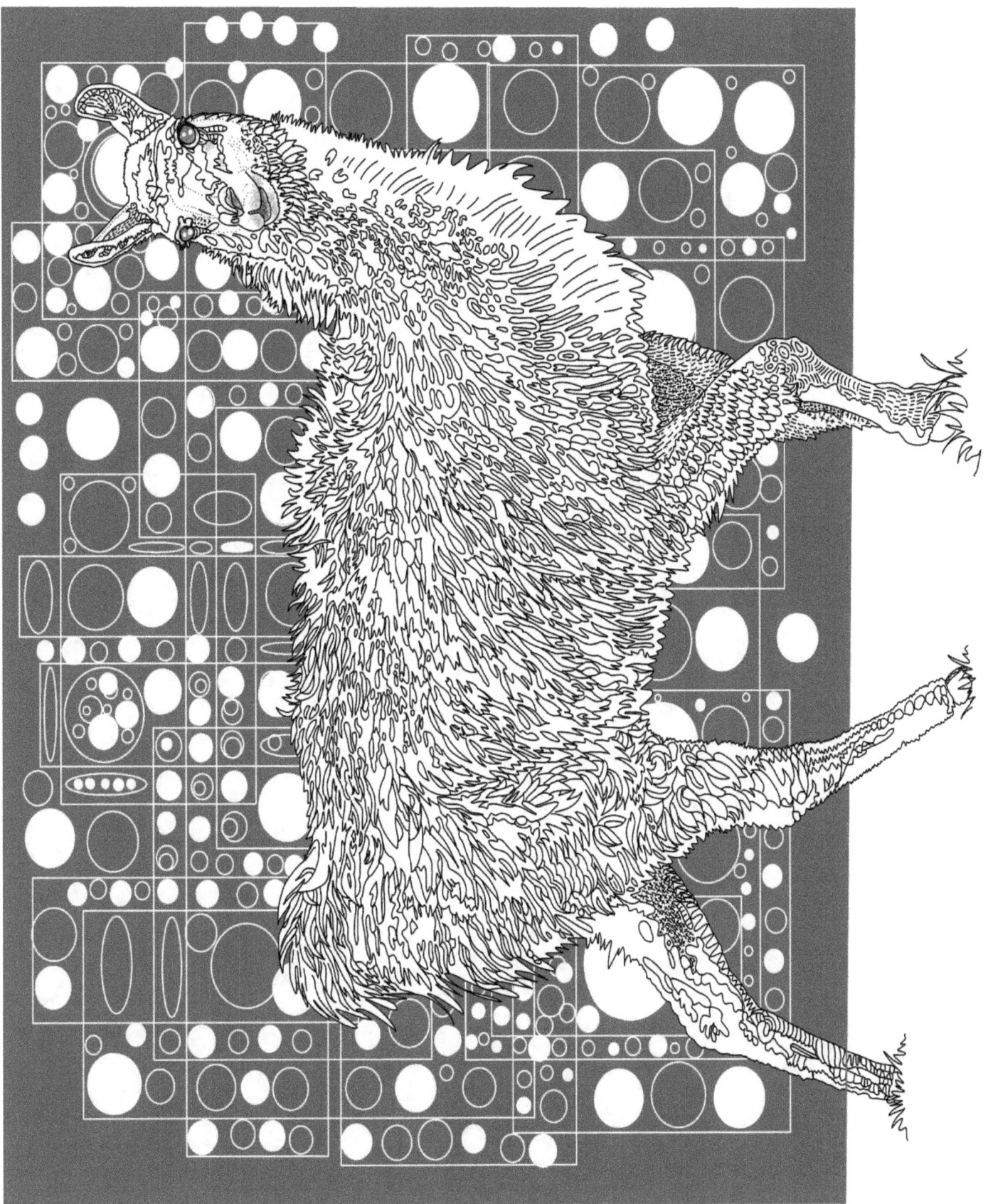

"COME, FLY WITH ME!" SAID THE HORSE. "BUT YOU RUN ON LEGS!" I SAID. "CLIMB UP, HOLD ON, YOU'LL SEE!" SAID HE. I DID, OF COURSE.

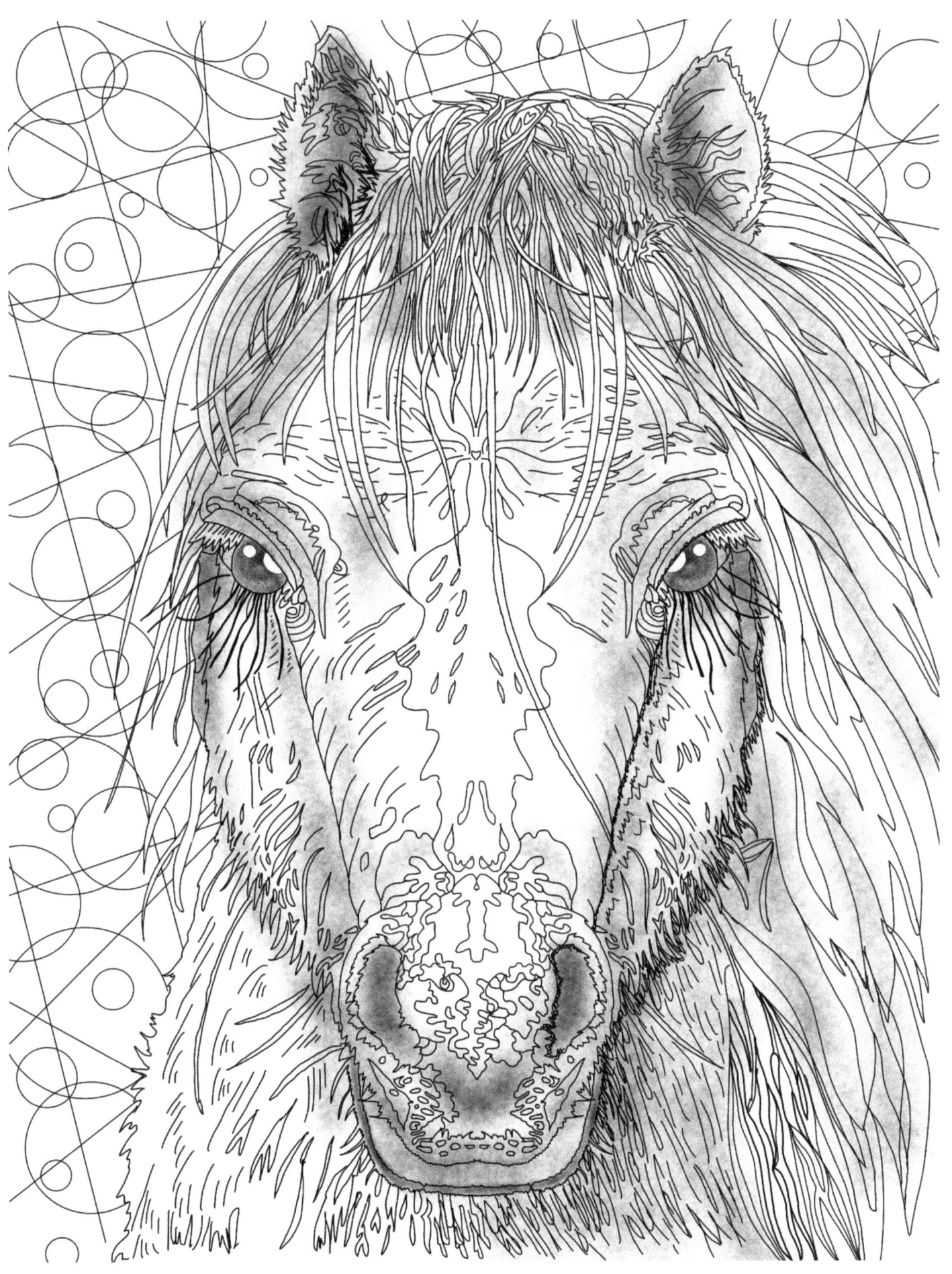

LAMBS WITH
WOOL AS SOFT
AS SILK,
HOW YOU LOVE
YOUR MOMMA'S
MILK.

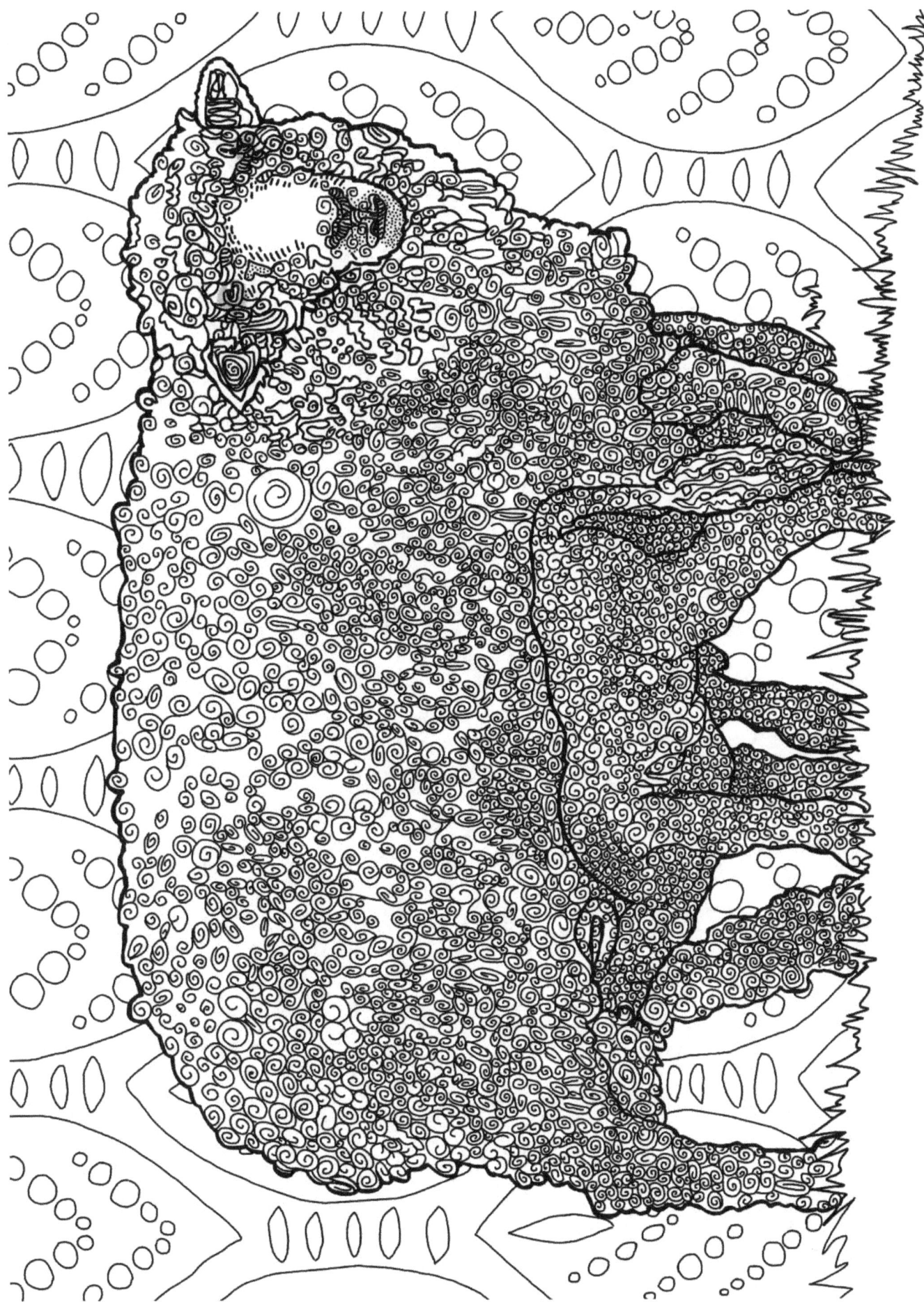

THE LION IS THE KING OF BEASTS! WHILE OTHERS FLEE, THE PRIDE WILL FEAST!

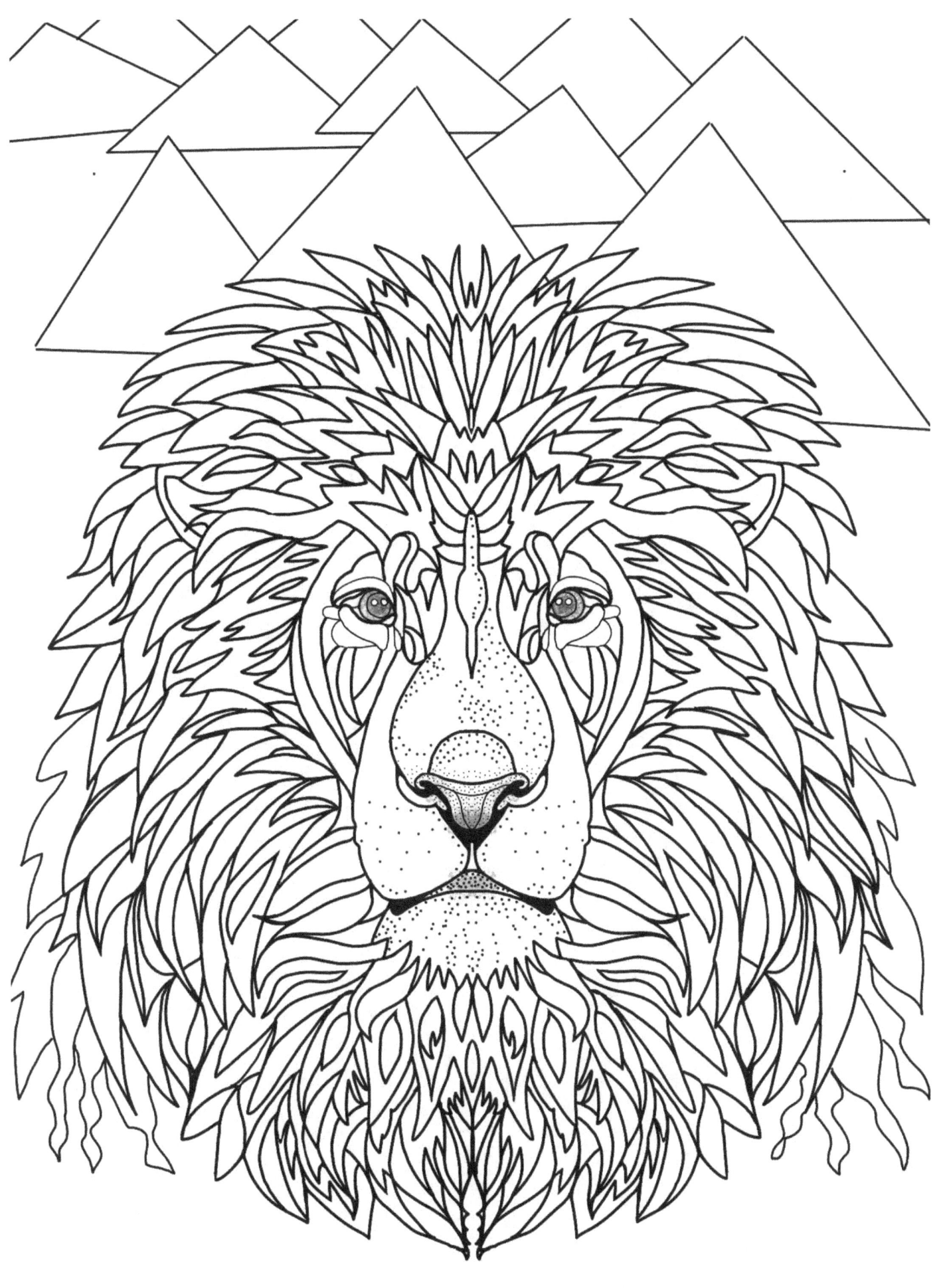

THE QIVIUT, WHO
DWELL IN THE
ARCTIC'S COLD,
ARE MILD,
SOBER FELLOWS,
OR SO I AM TOLD.

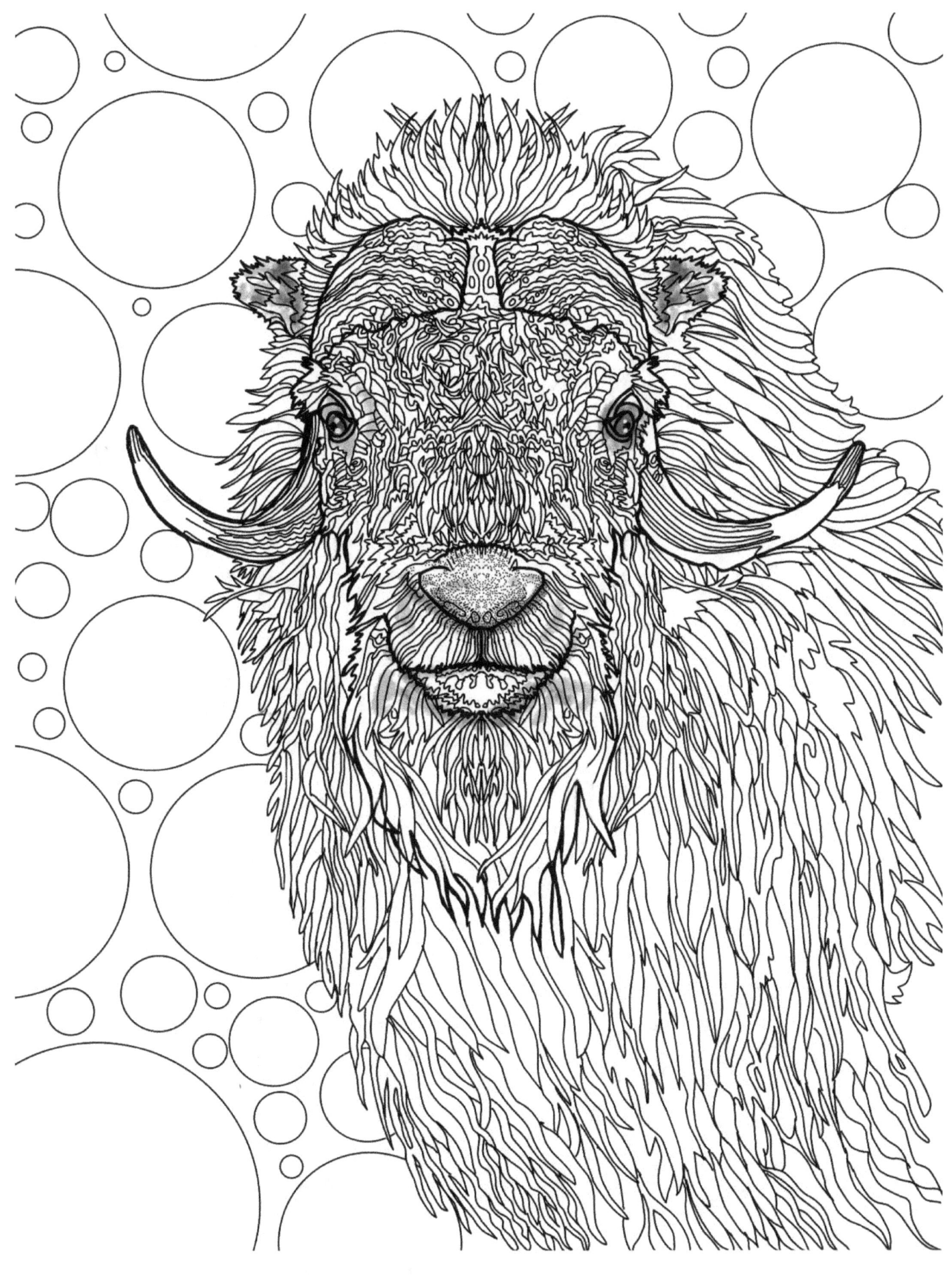

"BAA!", SAYS THE BLACK SHEEP, SHE HAS CURLY WOOL. SO DOES THE WHITE SHEEP, BIG BAGS·FULL.

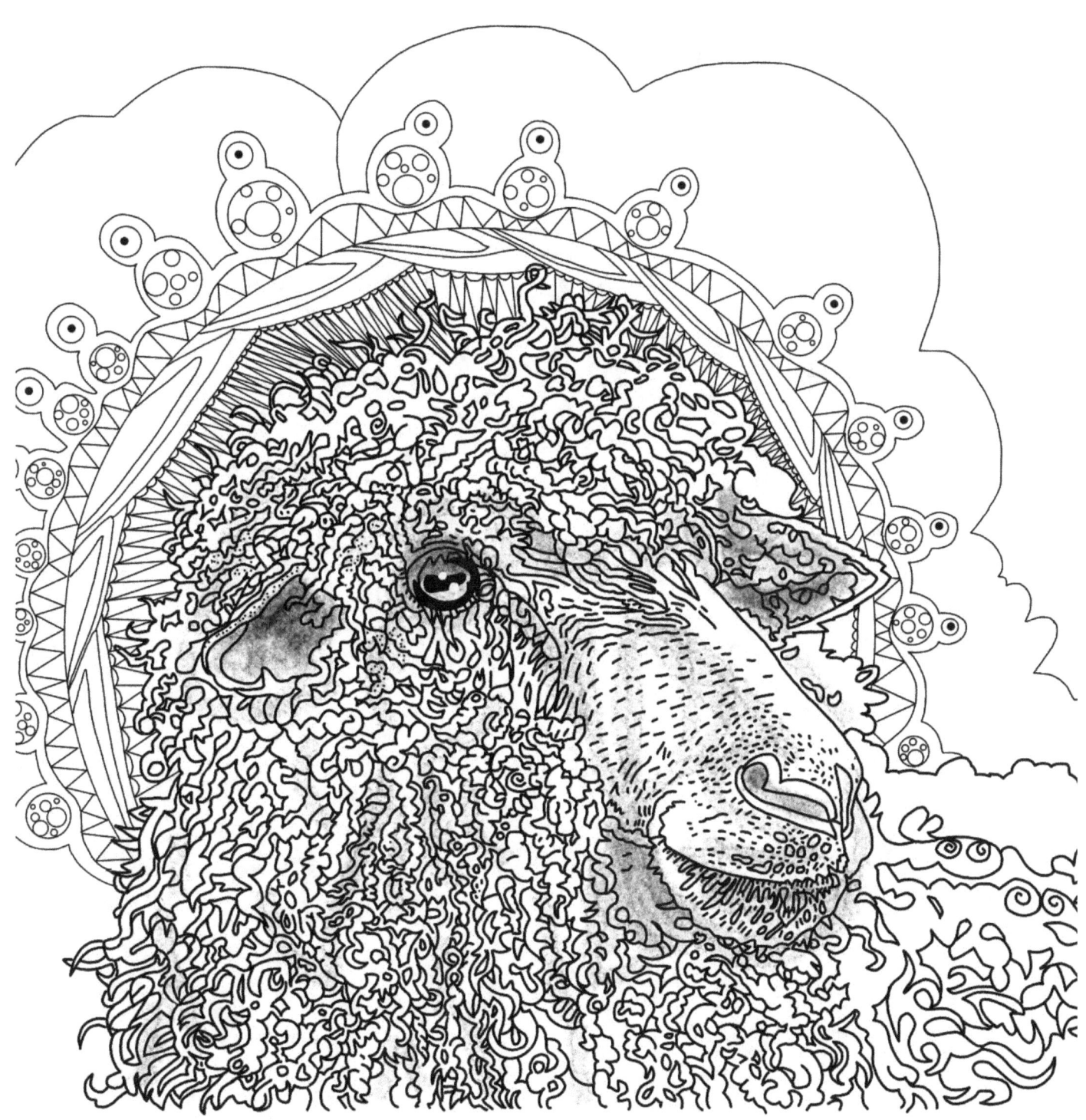

YAK YAK, YAKITTY YAK! YAK YAK, YAK YAK, YAK.

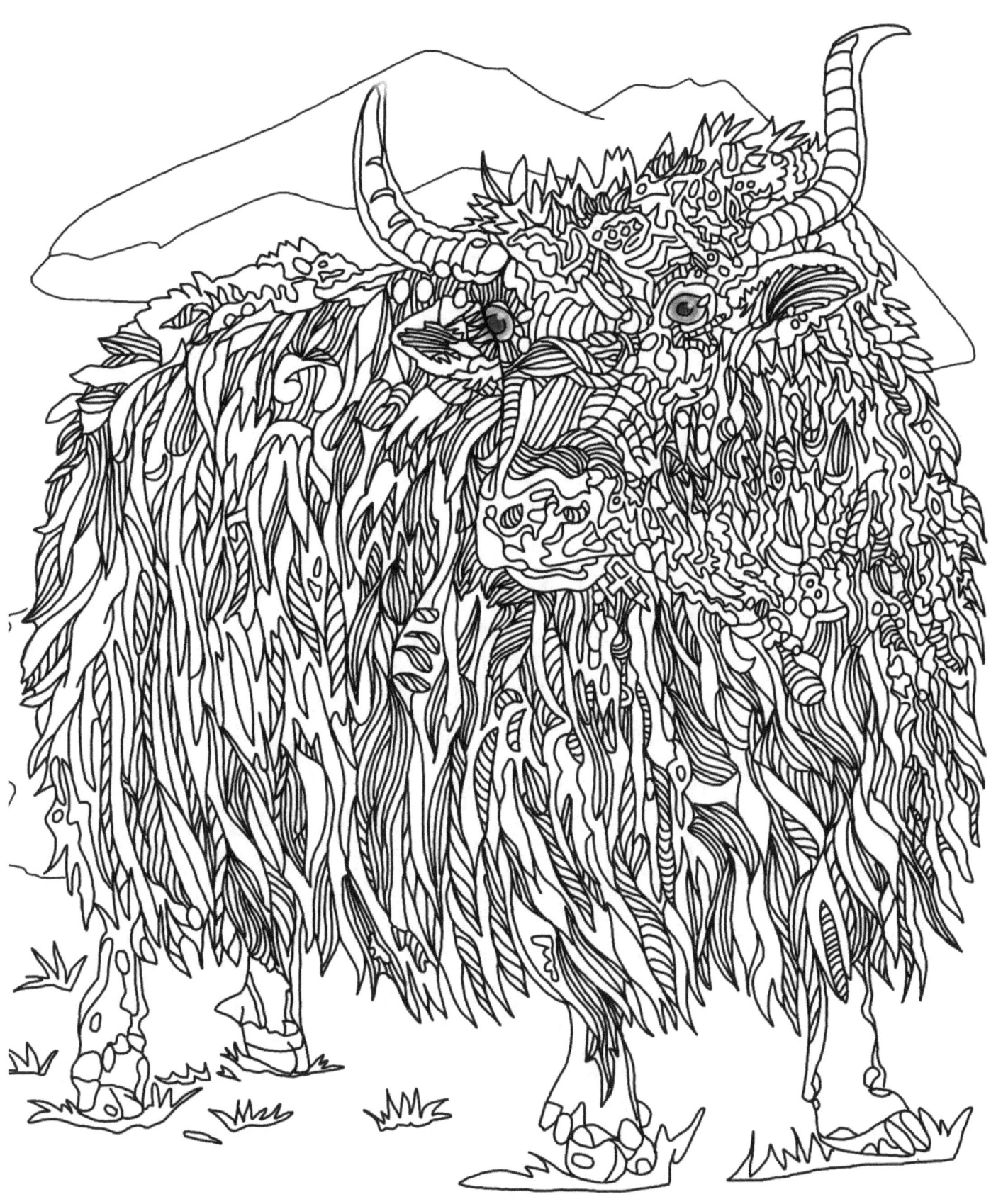